Thoughts
for Growi

Lionel Fanthorpe

Lionel & Patricia Fanthorpe

Patricia Fanthorpe

BISHOPSGATE PRESS

This book is dedicated to our much loved and admired friends Stan and Joyce Mogford, who continually help so many new Christians to grow.

British Library Cataloguing in Publication Data
Fanthorpe, Lionel and Patricia
Thoughts and Prayers for Growing Christians

All enquiries and requests relevant to this title should be sent to the publisher Bishopsgate Press Ltd., Bartholomew House, 15 Tonbridge Road, Hildenborough, Kent TN11 9BH.

Printed by Lanes Ltd.,
16 Patricia Way, Pysons Road Industrial Estate,
Broadstairs, Kent CT10 2LF.

Contents

Foreword

by Canon Stanley Mogford, MA

Much in life has something irresistible about it. There seem to be powers at work that have their way with us, and even act in spite of us.

The natural world provides evidence of it. Some birds seem capable of accepting captivity. Others, if set in a cage, will exhaust themselves beating against the bars. They are meant to be free and can bear nothing less.

Many plants or shrubs form a known shape, and to this shape, the power within them forces them to grow. If badly pruned, they will do all they can to redress the damage and revert to this created pattern. There are probably forces at work in nature that cannot easily be defied.

The human being also, in this respect at least, is as much part of the natural world as the skylark or the rose. There are just such forces at work in human nature and there, too, they cannot be denied.

There are forces within us that make us grow. We begin as tiny babies, weighing little and capable of being carried in one loving arm. Thereafter, we grow irresistibly. We can't hasten the process; nor can we stop it. The human being, sadly may retain the selfish, petulant nature of a child but he will have it in the body of a full grown man or woman.

There are forces within us that make us age. We may resist them all we can, and most of us do. We fight the flab. We fight the wrinkles. We fight the loss of memory. It will be all in vain. We have to surrender to age no matter what we do to resist it. Perhaps it will not be so fearsome as Shakespeare described it;

"Second childishness and mere oblivion, sans teeth, sans eyes, sans taste, sans everything"

But if we go to our full term, the process of ageing will show itself.

There are, in truth, forces at work in us that act in spite of us. They have control of us and we come to terms with them because we must.

One thing, at least, it seems, seldom, if ever, comes of itself. It is Goodness. It ought to be there for all of us, if we are God's children, the work of his Creative Hands, but sadly it is not. No one and nothing compels us to be patient, loving, kindly, generous, forgiving, gentle, understanding people. There are no powers at work inside us that compel us to any of these qualities. It may have made life easier and sweeter for many of us if there were. If they are to be part of us, we have to grow into them and we need all the help we can find if we are to succeed.

Some will find all the help they need within their family background. They will find there an example of love that never lets them go. Others will look to their families in vain, finding the background one of discord, and selfishness. Others, by chance or design, will find their help from friends whose way of life is kindly and where love of God and love of man never cease to comfort, strengthen and guide. Others, again by chance or design, choose companions whose pattern of life degrades and cheapens all they touch. It is all too easy to conform to the background of that circle. Inspiration to goodness can come from an inspired school, or an alert teacher. It can come from a chance acquaintance, whose intervention at a critical stage in life can never fully be repaid. It can come from a book as it did with St Augustine. He was told through words he heard from somewhere around him or inside him to take up the Bible and read. To him the words "Tolle, Lege" came like a shaft of lightning and the book hence forward guided his way through life.

All of us need guidance - even the cleverest and most devout of us. We need someone to encourage us when we feel depressed after failure, someone who will never allow us to be complacent and content with a troubled quality of life, who will take our Faith when it trembles and is fearful, and make it live for us again. Compulsion to goodness would be easier. But it doesn't happen and ought not to happen. God trusts us with our freedom. So we look for guidance whenever and wherever we can find it.

In and through this small book, the author, the Revered Lionel Fanthorpe tries to be that guide to us. He writes for all would-be Christians who as yet haven't made it. He has comfort for all dejected Christians who have lost their way. He has his own strength and faith to share with Christians who accept what they are expected to believe, but undermine it all by doubt. He writes not so much with his pen but with his heart. Every line is for someone. Those who long to root in the Faith, and grow in it, will come to Bless him for his lessons.

Canon Stanley Mogford
Cardiff, 2001

Introduction

When we teach our biology students about the seven classical attributes of living things, one of those vital attributes is the ability to grow. Babies and children do it so fast that it's almost a visible process. But we can all continue to improve and make progress right through this earthly life, whatever our age and however slowly we do it. We can also feel confident that this God-given process of development continues throughout the eternal and abundant life of Heaven which Christ came to bring us. It is an expression of God's infinite love for us that there is always something better ahead, something new and wonderful to which we can look forward with faith, hope and excitement.

Of course there are setbacks, problems and struggles. There are dark times and bitter disappointments. Life's road has its dangerous corners, steep hills and awkward diversions - but by the Grace of God we reach our Destiny in the end: and our Christian Destiny is everlasting joy with Christ and those whom we love.

There's a story about a lost traveller in the Rhondda who asked his way to Llanabercoed. A kindly Welsh farmer gave him the necessary but very complicated instructions about how to get there, and ended by saying thoughtfully: "If I was going to Llanabercoed, I wouldn't start from here."

Like that lost traveller, the new Christian has to start from wherever he or she may be. If we suddenly found ourselves standing ten feet below the summit of Mount Everest, climbing that last minute section wouldn't be much of an achievement. Crossing India, Tibet and Nepal on foot carrying all our own climbing gear before we actually tackled the Himalayas might be worth a diary entry or two.

Some of us are cradle Christians, born into loving Christian families where faith in God and service to Christ are as natural as the air we breathe. Others of us come in from outside. John Newton, the gifted and caring Parish Priest who wrote Amazing Grace was once a slave trader. Peter was a fisherman. Matthew was a tax collector. We start from wherever we happen to be when Christ calls us. Once the decision is made, the growing can start. Jesus Himself told the wonderfully relevant Parable of the Sower. The seed in that parable represents the Word of God. The types of soil into which it falls are the different kinds of people who hear God's call and respond to it in different ways. With God's help, we can be the right kind of soil for healthy and sustained Christian growth.

We can produce an eternal harvest of everlasting joy and abundant life.

What are the essential elements for Christian growth?

Firstly, there is love. If the meaning of the universe itself can be summed up in one word, that word is love. Love creates. Love sustains. Love endures forever. It is the quintessential nature of God - and God shares it with us. If we are to grow as Christians, we must learn to love other people in the same way that God loves us. We must set out positively to seek their happiness, for the giving of happiness to others is the surest expression of Christian love.

Secondly, there is faith. Christianity is a system of interwoven beliefs. It is not mathematics. It is not science. It is not logic. It is not law. It cannot be proved from any of those rigorous, academic perspectives. Faith lives and moves and has its being in the freedom of the human heart and spirit. Faith has its own strong, sound reasons, but they are qualitatively different from the proofs of mathematicians, scientists and judges. To grow in faith, we need to see what ordinary men and women have accomplished by their faith over the centuries. We can see the evidence of faith at work in other Christian lives, and in our own.

Thirdly, there is prayer. We need to listen very carefully and sensitively to the loving promptings of God, and then to open our hearts to him as we pray first for others and then for ourselves.

Fourthly, there is Bible reading and Bible study. We can learn so much from it, and grow as we read and learn.

Fifthly, there is Christian companionship and the corporate life of the Christian community. Because God loves us, He wants to be with us, and He wants us to be with one another in a strong, caring, mutually supportive, unselfish and loving group: His Church.

Sixthly, we grow by doing things, by participating, by sharing, by helping and by being as active as we can. The more we do for Christ, His Church and His people, the bigger and stronger Christians we become.

Seventhly, there is monitoring and self-appraisal. We need quiet moments to have a good look at ourselves, to evaluate our progress and to take whatever action is necessary to improve. We should never despair, and never be disappointed. God knows us infinitely better than we can ever hope to know ourselves. God loves us forever and to the ultimate -- Christ taught us that at Calvary. There are no lengths to which God will not go to help us. By ourselves we are nothing -- but with God we can solve every problem and overcome every obstacle.

Welcoming New Christians

Few things can equal the importance of a warm welcome. We shall always remember the way that Canon Jack Buttimore welcomed us to his Church of St David's in Ely near Cardiff when we came to Wales many years ago. Being made welcome by God's people is a great help and encouragement to new and growing Christians. But a welcome is a two way process: it calls for an appropriate response. There can be no doubt about the loving warmth of God's welcome. When Jesus told the parables of the Lost Sheep and the Prodigal Son (St Luke's Gospel, chapter 15) He revealed the infinite strength of God's love for the whole human race. There are no exclusions. There are no exceptions. God loves us all, and wants to welcome us all. Once we have accepted that divine invitation, we need to learn how to respond to God's welcome - and the best response to a warm and loving welcome is gratitude for it. Being grateful to God, and showing that gratitude to God's people, is an important stage in our Christian growth.

Welcome Poem

When God invites His children in, no power can close the door,
And what God welcomes us to share is Life forever more.
The Cross stood high on Calvary to show us all the way.
The Light of Christ shall guide us through to God's Eternal Day
There is no clearer welcome, than God's welcome for the lost.
He does not grudge the gifts he gives. He never counts the cost.
Though we are new ourselves, great Lord, teach us to welcome others,
And tell the world how much you love our sisters and our brothers.

Prayer of Welcome

Thank You, Lord of Love, for the welcome I received when I first turned to You. Help me to respond to Your love with all my strength, and to offer a welcome to those who are seeking You now, as I was then. Help me to understand my brothers and sisters in Christ, and to learn to work with them in the fellowship and companionship of Your Church. Help me to be part of the team that makes others welcome in Your Name. Grant me the grace to live my new Christian life in such a fulfilled and useful way that everything I do and say will help others to find Your Welcome, for Jesus' sake,

Amen.

Thinking About God

As growing Christians, we realise that God Himself is the Divine Environment in which we grow. We are also growing in certain positive directions: towards love, towards fellowship and towards an eternal joy that is an infinite distance beyond our present understanding. All of these things are God's gifts. As we try to think about Him, so we begin to grow more purposefully and assuredly. Even though the Being and Nature of God are far beyond our present earthly comprehension, one of the best and most important things we can do is to think about Him. St Paul was blessed with rich spiritual understanding and great wisdom. He tells us plainly enough to think about things that are good, true, pure, lovely and of good report. Nothing is better, truer, or purer than God - so there is no better direction for the growing Christian's thoughts. One of the most useful ways of directing our thoughts towards God is to think first about everything good that we enjoy during our time on this earth. God is more to be loved and admired than the finest and most beautiful things we have ever experienced here. The kindest and most loving human being we have ever met is only the palest reflection, the faintest shadow, of God's perfect love. We can think of God as the True and Original Source of all that is good -- both Giver and Sustainer.

Thinking of God

We see you in Creation, Lord, and seeing You, we grow.
You made the stellar universe - each flake of falling snow.
You made the distant galaxies - and graceful larks that sing.
Your hands engraved each tiny line on every insect's wing.
We read Your plan in history, and the great ocean swell,
We hear your love in children's prayers and in the
evening bell.
Your gifts inspire the artist's hand. You guide the poet's pen.
You are the God of Everywhere, the Lord of Everywhen.
You made the Universal Laws that Scientists explore.
You are the God of fearless hearts who seek a distant shore.
And though we cannot comprehend a fraction of your love
Grant us the grace to grow until we meet with You above.

A Prayer of Contemplation

Eternal and almighty Lord, You are infinitely farther away from this tiny planet than the most distant star on the edge of the universe. Yet You are also closer to us than the air we breathe and those on this earth whom we love most. Help us, O Lord, to contemplate the awesome size, and the amazing smallness which You have given us in creation. Teach us our rightful place as stewards and guardians of this beautiful natural word -- and help us to see You in it. Give our minds the strength and courage to examine what has been written and preached about Your Truth, and help us to find the time, the quietness and the perfect place in which to meditate upon it, for the sake of Christ our Lord.
Amen.

Jesus

The unique element in our Christian faith which singles it out from the other great world religions is the Person and Character of our Lord Jesus Christ, the Carpenter from Nazareth. As Christians we believe that His birth at Bethlehem on the First Christmas Day was one of the three most important events in world history. His death on the cross and His resurrection were the second. His return in glory will be the third. In Jesus, God Himself became human. In Jesus, God broke into human history and changed it irreversibly for the better. In and through Jesus and his work on earth for our sakes, God bestowed the gift of eternal and abundant life on all who are willing to accept His invitation. This is the centre of our Christian faith. Jesus, the Son of God, is both fully human and fully divine.

In all that He said and did during His incarnation, Jesus radiated the love of God. His parables taught us about the mercy and forgiveness of God. His life provided us with the most perfect possible example of how a human life ought to be lived. Above all He provides us, as growing Christians, with a picture of what we should all aim to be, for His sake. He gives us the strength to grow to be what He wants us to be. Yet He also wants us to be free, to be independent, and to be truly *ourselves*.

Jesus

In Christ we find the perfect Way,
The Life, the Truth, the Light,
And as we follow where He leads,
We say farewell to night.
No darkness can obscure our path
When Jesus leads the way.
He takes us to eternal joy
And Heaven's endless day.
For He once dwelt where we now dwell
And made this Earth His home:
As Perfect God and Perfect Man
Among us He did roam.
He has endured our suffering,
And He has borne our pain,
So we shall share His boundless joy
When He comes back again.

Prayer

Lord Jesus Christ, You are at the very heart of our Christian faith. You are our Leader, our Example and our Guide. You walked this earth as Perfect God and Perfect Man. You died for us on the Cross. You rose in glorious victory, the Conqueror of Sin and Death. Teach us what You want us to be. Help us to serve You to the best of our ability, to grow into the kinds of Christian men and women that You would have us be. Inspire us and empower us, so that as we grow in the faith, we may learn to express our love for You by loving, serving and caring for others.
Amen.

The Holy Spirit

The Holy Spirit is the Third Person of the Trinity. His limitless power and might are like those of the Father and the Son. Yet each Person of the Holy Trinity is separate as well as united, in a way that even the oldest, the wisest and the most scholarly of Christians cannot really begin to understand. Simply because the human mind cannot comprehend the great mystery of God's Supra-personal Triune Nature, we have no excuse for failing to recognise the presence and work of the Holy Spirit in the world, in us, and in the people around us. Whatever is good, whatever is kind, whatever is generous and unselfish is the work of the Holy Spirit's prompting. The best, the kindest, the most generous and unselfish men and women owe all that is best in them to the work of the Holy Spirit. When we listen to Him, and go in the direction in which He is directing us, untold good comes of it. When we are as stubborn as mules, and as self-centred as only human beings seem to know how to be, all the good that we could have achieved in that particular set of circumstances is hindered and delayed. It's not lost, it's only interrupted and held back for a while. The Holy Spirit's power and love can never be defeated. He will bring us to what is best for us - no matter how difficult we make His task by our weakness and selfishness.

The Holy Spirit

Father, Son and Holy Spirit, God of Perfect Unity,
Indivisible but separate, Lord of Triune Majesty,
God of glory, God of mystery, far beyond all human thought,
Help us, teach us and inspire us: may we love You as we ought.
Holy Spirit, dwell among us, dwell within us and around,
Where your presence works its wonders, truth and love and joy are found.
Heal the sick and lead the wayward back towards the Father's care.
Strengthen those who seek to serve You; help us all to give and share.
Guard and guide us, Holy Spirit, lead us everywhere we go.
Teach us how to serve and please You: aid us as we seek to grow.

Prayer for the Holy Spirit's Guidance

Be with us, Holy Spirit of God, to lead us, to guard us, to comfort and protect us in everything we do, and in every place we go. Strengthen us so that we can help others. Show us the way, so that we can lead others to God. Grant us the light of your wisdom so that we can understand the divine truth contained in the Scriptures. Teach us, so that we may help others to learn. Give us the valour to speak boldly for Christ when forthright courage is needed. Grant us the wisdom and endurance to wait in silence, when calmness and patience are needed. Help us to grow in faith, in knowledge and in love to God and to our brothers and sisters. We ask it in the Name of Jesus our Lord.
Amen.

Going to Church

One of our favourite stories - and it may well be true - concerns a lady who found that a visiting Bishop was hearing confession in her church that day because her Parish Priest was away. This made her so nervous that she couldn't think of anything to confess, except to admit that although she loved God and her fellow beings she found church services boring. "So do I, my dear little sister, so do I," chuckled the Bishop. "I only attend because I'm a Bishop!" He went on to say that while he fully shared her love of God and humanity, the actual church services themselves seemed unbearably dull and pointless to him. If that story has a basis in fact, both the Bishop and the parishioner are to be warmly commended for their honesty. But church services needn't be dull, lifeless and boring. There are churches which make prayer, worship and Christian fellowship more enjoyable and exciting than a Cup Tie, a Wimbledon Final or a West End musical. We're all different. God made us so. There will be a church in your area which fulfils all your growing Christian hopes. Don't be afraid to visit several until you find one which you feel will be a real spiritual home for you. Be true to yourself in your choice of a church. God prizes honesty and individuality.

The Church I Want

I'd like to find a church where friends can meet,
Where fellowship abounds, and we can greet
Each other warmly by the open door,
Where children play and romp across God's floor.

I don't like silence, rigidly enforced,
Or detailed rules punctiliously endorsed.
I don't like classic choirs - they're too precise --
Nor anthems where each line's repeated twice.

I don't like frameworks, liturgies nor creeds:
Freedom of worship satisfies my needs.
We each should seek the church that suits us best:
God's love and mercy will provide the rest.

Prayer for the Church

Loving Lord, You are the Head of the whole Church, help us to find a church where we can worship You in spirit and in truth. Help us to analyse our own personal needs with complete honesty, choosing what is right for us, not what we think other people expect us to do. Help us to find You in and through the work and worship of the church we attend. Grant us the grace to participate to the best of our ability in those areas of church life where we can be useful. Lord, help us to find a church where we can grow as Christians, and where we can help others to grow, a church where there is joyful fellowship, and where all who attend can really feel that we are part of one great loving and supportive family. We ask it in the Name of Christ our Lord.
Amen.

The Christian at Work

Saint Paul set us a great example - he worked as a tent-maker, and paid his own way when he went on long, arduous, missionary journeys. Many excellent non-stipendiary Priests and voluntary Ministers and Pastors today follow Saint Paul's example. Some are police officers, others are solicitors, some work in medicine or engineering. Lionel, for example, is a professional actor and entertainer, a regular radio and TV performer, and a fully paid-up member of Equity. Patricia's his Agent and Manager as well as his wife. Christians find themselves earning their livings in all sorts of ways in this complex modern world. Whether we earn our daily bread as brain surgeons or shop assistants, Members of Parliament or musicians, God wants us to give a fair day's work for a fair day's pay. It can sometimes be difficult to be a Christian in the working environment, but Christ understands those difficulties. He was a working man himself. His disciples were working men too. When we take our work problems to Him in prayer we can be totally confident that He knows all about them and sympathises with our difficulties. The Prophet Amos was a simple herdsman from the hills of Tekoa. He worked hard for small rewards, and so he understood the importance of fairness and justice at work. Amos, like St Paul, is well worth copying.

Working for God

Though it's some great multi-national
Signs the pay-checks that I draw,
When I answer to my conscience
Then it's God I'm working for.

He's the finest of Employers.
He is merciful and kind,
But He sets the highest standards
And we must not fall behind.

We are sent to serve His people
So His Truth can be revealed
But He needs a host more workers
In this human harvest field.

We are following the pathway
Which our Lord and Saviour trod.
We are here to serve our neighbours:
We are here to work for God.

A Working Prayer

Loving and caring Lord Jesus Christ, during your earthly incarnation as one of us, You knew what it was like to work hard for a long time and to be in need of rest. Help us to work to the best of our ability, whatever our job may be. Make us honest, truthful, responsible and reliable in our work, so that by the way we do our job we can show our Christian standards. Help us, as Amos the Prophet taught, to give good value and good service. Help us to work at being good Christians - as well as being good Christians at work. Help us to grow in the Christian skills of love, gentleness, mercy and peace, kindness and generosity, just as we seek to grow in our professional, technical or administrative skills at work. We ask it in and through your precious Name. Amen.

The Christian at Home

A loving Christian home is the greatest blessing any of us can ever hope to receive on this Earth. In the true and unselfish love of husbands and wives, parents and children, brothers and sisters, grandparents, grandchildren, aunts, uncles, nephews, nieces and cousins we see pale reflections, or distant gleamings, of the radiant and limitless love of God. To be in love is to be truly alive. Rejoicing in the company of those who mean much more to us than our own existence is a faint echo of the eternal and abundant rejoicing of the Saints and Angels above. The Christian at home is as close to Heaven as he or she can get before Christ calls us to our eternal home with Him, and with all those we love who have gone ahead of us. We need to make the most of our homes, and especially of the wonderful family members who share them with us. Never worry about what the place looks like. Love and kindness, mutual appreciation, comfort, encouragement, help and support are the richest and most beautiful furnishings. God is the Head of every Christian home, and Jesus Himself was cradled in the manger in Bethlehem when He came to make His home with us on Earth. The Christian home is also a place of welcoming, giving and sharing - never turn the needy away.

Home

When the days are long and weary,
And the toiling has no end,
Home is where we find renewal
With a loved one or a friend.

Home is where we pray together.
Home is where we help and share,
Bearing one another's burdens:
Time to listen, time to care.

Home's the haven we relax in:
Watch TV, and play or read.
Home's the place to be together
With the families we need.

Prayers at Home

Lord, teach us to value all those we love who share our homes with us. Help us to see that the youngest and the oldest, the biggest and the smallest, all have their special contributions to make. Remind us to be grateful, and never to take the people we love for granted. Join in our games as well as in our prayers and worship at home. Help us always to remember that You are the true Head of every household, and that Your rule is a rule of caring and sharing love. As we love our own children, and delight when they are at home with us, remind us that we are all Your children, and that the most acceptable form of worship is to show kindness and love to others. We ask it in the Name of Jesus Christ our Lord.
Amen.

The Meaning of Marriage and Baptism

There are many significant milestones and landmarks in the life of the growing Christian: marriage and baptism are two of them. The outward forms of baptism may change from one Christian group to another, but its essential inner meaning is the same everywhere. By being baptised into the Christian faith, we are becoming members of Christ's Church, part of the great Christian family stretching back 2000 years, and spreading across the whole of God's world. Just as the age of a great tree is marked by its rings, so these Christian centuries are marked by the lives of the faithful. The apostles and saints whose lives marked out the first few Christian centuries were baptised and married. Their lives had Christian landmarks too.

In marriage, two loving Christians unite as the foundation of a new Christian family. Jesus Himself blessed the wedding at Cana of Galilee, and came to the rescue of the deeply embarrassed host when the wine ran out before the celebrations were completed. The joy of being permanently united to a deeply loving partner is yet another living symbol of the way that God loves all of us. As marriage partners grow in love over the years, so the growing Christian grows closer and closer to the divine and eternal love of God.

Baptism and Marriage Poem

Two milestones on the growing Christian's way:
Landmarks that point towards eternal day --
In Baptism we boldly mark the start
Of life with Christ that stirs the loving heart.
In married bliss with someone whom we love
We see reflections of the joy above.

Lord, mark for us the road which leads to You,
With sacred moments, and with guidance true
Lead on from our Baptismal promise till
We see the radiance of Your heavenly hill.
Bless every good commitment that we make
And help us, Lord, to keep them for Your sake.

A Prayer of Growing Commitment

Most loving God of perfect truth and absolute integrity, help us to keep the solemn promises we make in Baptism and Marriage. Strengthen our many human weaknesses so that we may always do the good that we strive to do, and shun the evil which seeks to lure us away from You, from truth and from goodness. Help us, as we grow in the faith of Christ, to defend all that is good and right, and to condemn all that hurts, betrays or exploits others. Show us again, Lord, the unbreakable commitment which led Jesus to Calvary's cross for us, and enrich us with a share of His unconquerable strength and absolute determination, so that we may serve Your people for His sake.

Amen.

Fellowship Groups

Christianity is the finest and most exciting of all team games. As we grow in the faith, and become more experienced in God's service, so we come to recognise our need of other Christians more and more. When we meet together it strengthens and encourages us all. When we gather in fellowship groups in our churches and in our homes, we learn about the gifts which God has given to our friends and companions, and we benefit greatly from being able to share in their blessings. Some can read the Scriptures aloud for the rest of us with such clarity and expression that they come alive in a new and special way. Others are inspired to sing hymns or play musical instruments so well that the quality of their music brings us closer to God. Some have the Lord's gift of leading us in prayer, or preaching uplifting sermons. Some tend the sick, visit prisoners, lead youth clubs -- or drive and maintain the church minibus. We are all individuals, but we're also part of God's great plan. He loves us as individuals, and He loves us for being totally free, independent and true to ourselves - but He also wants us to share those unique personalities and gifts which he has bestowed upon each one of us so that working lovingly together in His service we can achieve far more than we could hope to do alone. Fellowship is just as important as individuality.

Fellowship

As the engine suits the body and the chassis fits the car,
They must work in perfect harmony, or else it won't go far,
So we all need one another as we strive to serve the Lord.
Our sisters' and our brothers' gifts must never be ignored.
Every one of them is precious, every one of them unique,
Every one of us is needed, and together we must seek
For the lost and for the lonely, for the ones of who've gone astray,
But unless we work in fellowship we'll never find the way.
Jesus loves each individual, and He made us what we are,
Yet He wants us all united - and our difference is no bar.
As He taught His first Disciples, so His truth lives with us still:
It's in fellowship ***together*** that we do the Father's will.

Prayer of Fellowship

We thank and praise You, great Lord of love and fellowship, for the good companions, the brothers and sisters in Christ, whom You have sent to help us and to work with us. Teach us all to understand and sympathise with one another's individual differences, to respect them, and to see that by uniting in fellowship, as a committed Christian team, we can serve You and Your world more effectively. Help us to grow together as we learn more of Your loving purpose for the universe that You have created, and which You sustain with Your eternal and unfailing power. We ask it in the Name of Jesus Christ our Lord.
Amen.

Christian Charity

Lord Jesus, when You came to Earth as a tiny, helpless babe in Mary's loving arms in the stable in Bethlehem, You gave us everything You had. You left the glory and wonder of Heaven to live as one of us here on Earth. You knew our needs, and You gave regardless of the cost until those needs were met. We learn so much from You as we grow in the faith. We learn the true meaning of Christian charity; we learn from You to give more than is asked, and we learn to go the second mile. Help us to grow in generosity and to be cheerful, willing givers for your sake. Housing the homeless, feeding the hungry, healing the sick and sparing time to be with the sad and lonely is infinitely important to You. Help us to grow as Christians until it becomes infinitely important to us as well. Help us to learn that giving our time is as important as giving our money. Teach us that giving our skills and special knowledge is as important as giving our time. Show us, through Christ's glorious and perfect example, that the truest and most acceptable form of charity consists of giving our friendship and love to those who are friendless and unloved. Help us also to remember that our Christian charity begins at home, within the Christian family, and that the more love and generosity we give there, the more effective givers we shall be in the outside world.

Charity

When all my obligations have been met,
And loved ones who depend on me are fed,
Then, Lord of Charity, be with me yet:
Help me to give the poor their daily bread.

When I have paid the bills that must be paid,
Done everything I promised would be done,
When I have honoured every contract made,
Then help me, Lord, to make this extra one:

Whatever I have left, when all is cleared --
Mine to dispose of in my chosen way --
When through torn veils of selfishness I've peered,
Let my small gift enrich another's day.

The Prayer of Charity

Lord, You give us everything. We have nothing of our own. The richest of us are only poor and unworthy stewards of your universal wealth. Grant us a true perspective on our earthly possessions, whether they be great or small. Give us the common sense and skill to use them wisely and sensibly, and never to confuse generosity with folly and rashness. Teach us to be prudent, careful and thrifty with what we have, so that we can guard those who depend upon us, but help us after that to use what we can rightly spare to aid those of your children who are in the greatest need. We ask it in the Name of Christ our Lord.
Amen.

Getting Involved

Some of the best, the kindest, the most loving and helpful people we have ever met have had a deep-seated fear of getting involved. It's an almost clinical phobia like the fear of heights or the fear of being in enclosed spaces. It's the very sensible and understandable fear that commitment of any kind tends to reduce our freedom - and freedom is a very precious commodity. God Himself recognises its supreme value because He gave us our freedom in the first place. It's something He wants us to have -- and to keep forever. Whatever seeks to limit it, or take it from us, is not from God. As growing Christians we need to be particularly wary of those who seek to impose rules, restrictions, orders and regulations upon us in the name of religion. Such trivial rubbish is a million miles from the eternal love and perfect freedom which Christ came to bring. But there are some things in which we have to get involved - no matter how fiercely, and how rightly, we feel the need to fight for our freedom. We have to be involved with our families: husbands, wives, sons and daughters, parents and grandparents. We have to be involved with those in need. We have to be involved with other members of Christ's team who are working with us to help the needy. We have to be involved with those who are looking for Christ and who want to ask us the way.

Getting Involved

Freedom, Lord, and independence,
These are what I value most.
God, I fear too much involvement:
I'm an island - not the coast.

Help me, Lord, defend my freedom --
Individuality --
Yet I know that there are places
Where my friends need me to be.

Somewhere there must be a balance -
Help me, Lord, to understand,
I must yield some of my freedom -
Give and take a helping hand.

Then the load will be much lighter,
And some problems be resolved.
Make me, Lord, a good team member:
Teach me how to get involved.

Prayer of Involvement

Loving Father, You have always been involved in loving and sustaining your creation. Christ your Son became one of us, and was totally involved with us, in order to help us and bring us to eternal and abundant life. In Him You set us the absolute and perfect example of involvement. Help us to overcome our hesitation and reluctance. Teach us, as we grow in the faith, how to become increasingly involved with all our brothers and sisters who are striving to help those in need. Make us into good members of the Christian team, so that through our involvement in your work, we may ease the suffering and distress of all in need. We ask it in the Name of Him Who involved Himself so totally with us, Jesus Christ our Lord.
Amen.

As we grow in our Christian faith and learn more about its privileges and responsibilities -- as well as the demands it makes on us - we take a new look at our place in the world as followers of Jesus. There are two extremes which we need to avoid. The first error is the harsh Puritanical approach that lumps "the world, the flesh and the devil" into one dangerously toxic bundle, and wrongly equates every innocent, God-given human pleasure with sin and its consequences. Always remember that the God you have begun to serve is a God of love. Above all, He wants you to be *happy,* and He wants you and all those whom you love to be with Him and to enjoy abundant life forever. He created you in order to show His love for you and to make you indescribably joyful eternally: that is truly and exactly what God's Love does. There are innumerable good gifts in this world which God has made for us. He put us all here to *enjoy* them. We're not meant to turn away from them, and pretend that they're bad for us. They are not. Innocent pleasure is as important as prayer and worship. ***God loves to see us happy***. The opposite error is that of the child so engrossed in the toy, that he or she ignores the loving parent or friend who gave it. Treat all the Earth's good things as gateways to God, and you will achieve perfect Christian balance in the world.

God's World and Ours

This is God's world and ours - no doubts on that -
Though evil longs to claim it,
It cannot.
Christ's power -
Impenetrable as a wall of steel --
Surrounds us and His world,
And we may feel
Eternally secure within His love.

So in His mighty Name we can attack
That darkness, which His glorious light hurls back.
We can proclaim God's justice, joy and love,
Until our world reflects His World above.

Prayer

God of love, joy and fellowship, show us that this wonderful world which You have made for us is a place which You intend us to enjoy. As we grow in our Christian faith, help us to grow in happiness. Show us that the surest way to enjoy our lives here on Earth is to share them with those in need. We ask it in the name of Christ our Lord. Amen.

Bible Study

The Bible is a fathomless mine of priceless spiritual treasure - but like all mines, it has to be treated with respect. To wrench a text out of its context and treat it as a pretext is not the way for the growing Christian to learn more of God's love and God's sacred laws. The unfailing Light by which we can best read the Bible is Christ. If we think consistently of what Jesus revealed to us about God His Father as we read, then our Bible reading will inspire and strengthen us as we grow in faith. The Bible describes Christ's life and work most vividly in the sublime Gospel of St John, and that's the starting point we recommend to all growing Christians. Always make Bible reading part of your life - but always make Christ's compassion and love part of your Bible reading.

Bible Poem

Read the Book carefully,
Thoughtfully, prayerfully.
Always let Christ light
The page as you read.

Remember Him stressing all
God's love and blessing all
Those who show kindness
To people in need.

Read in God's morning light,
So each day's dawning light
Helps us grow stronger
In thought, word and deed.

Read as the shadows fall:
All God's good gifts recall.
From fear and doubt then
Our minds will be freed.

Bible Study Prayer

We thank you, Lord, for all the truth, beauty and wisdom contained in the Bible. Help us to read it in the light of Christ, and may all that we learn from it help us to grow closer to Him. We ask it in and through His precious name.
Amen.

Prayer

Prayer is as important for the growing Christian as protein is for the growing athlete. The Christian life is built of prayers as surely as churches and chapels are built of bricks, mortar and stone. In prayer we listen to God. In prayer we offer our praise and thanks to God. In prayer we bring our petitions to God.

But Christ also taught us about the ***power*** of prayer, just as He taught us about the ***power*** of faith.

Prayer and faith together are the ingredients of that spiritual dynamite which can move mountains. Christ set us the perfect example in His own ideal prayer life and He also taught us to pray.

As Tennyson says: *More things are wrought by prayer than this world dreams of.*

Prayer Poem

When the day is filled with glory
And you've happiness to share,
Then thank God for all His goodness
And express those thanks in prayer.

When the storm clouds gather round you
And the day is dark as night
Turn to God in prayer and ask Him
For more strength with which to fight.

We can talk to Him and tell Him
Of each worry, strain and care.
And His heart is always open
To the faintest human prayer.

Prayer about Prayer

Lord of love and life, You have taught us through Christ Your Son that we should always come to You in prayer. Help us to pray meaningfully and from our hearts so that our prayers will always reach You. Help us to open our hearts and learn to listen to You in prayer. We ask it in the Name of Christ our Lord, whose life was always filled with prayer.
Amen

The Christian Conscience

Elijah the Prophet found God in "the still, small voice" and that's as good a description of conscience as any. As growing Christians we need to listen to that quiet, gentle, inner voice at all times. We need to be guided by it in all that we think, say and do, but just like our Bible reading, the promptings of conscience need to be treated with careful thought and prayer.

Some tragic, mentally ill criminals have claimed that they were urged to commit their brutal acts because of some "inner voice" that urged them on. Unless our "inner voice" - our conscience - prompts us to be kind, loving, tolerant and merciful, we should regard it with extreme caution. While listening attentively to the common sense counsel of a conscience that is in harmony with Christ's teaching and example on all life's big issues, we need to guard against the problems of the hypersensitive conscience - the kind which worries for hours over what to do about a 5 pence piece found on a bus seat.

Conscience Poem

(Fanthorpean Sonnet Form)

Our conscience is that still small voice within
Which prompts right actions and denounces sin.
Our conscience is the gauge from which we read
The moral value of each word and deed.
Our conscience is the compass, clear and bright,
Which points to Christ and guides our steps aright.
Our conscience is the star by which we steer -
Whose brightness shows that God Himself is near.
Our conscience is that beam of inner light
Which shines to aid our inward moral sight.
Our conscience is the silver bell we need
To ring its warnings against self and greed.
Our conscience points to where we must begin --
And through life's battles, conscience helps us win.

Conscience Prayer

Perfect and righteous God of truth, fairness and justice, help us to listen prayerfully and carefully to the quiet, inner voice of conscience, which you have given to help and guide us. Grant us the judgement and wisdom to decide which of those inner promptings are in harmony with your eternal and immutable Law of Love, and help us to act on them. Amen.

Faith

We all need faith - growing Christian and mature ones alike - and faith in turn needs *reason*. It also needs action because *faith without works is dead*.

The essential outlines of our faith can be found in the creeds which the various branches and denominations of God's Church use. These can be condensed into the creating and sustaining power of God; the unique work of reconciliation achieved by Jesus His Son during His incarnation in the Holy Land 2,000 years ago; the strengthening and inspiring power of the ever present Holy Spirit and the eternal, abundant and unimaginably joyful future which follows this earthly life.

God's law can be summed up in the one word: ***love***. His love for us, our love for Him - and for one another. This is our Christian faith. By this we live. In this we grow. Through this we transcend suffering and death and go on to an endless future of joy beyond our wildest dreams.

Faith

Father, Son and Holy Spirit,
God of life and God of love.
Lord of justice, Lord of mercy,
Lord of Earth and Heaven above.
In this faith we kneel and worship.
On this faith our lives we base.
Guard and guide us on faith's journey -
Till we see You face to face.

The Prayer of Faith

Lord, help us to grow in faith. Show us that you are always with us. Remind us constantly of your infinite power which built this universe and now sustains it. Grant us unswerving and unwavering faith in Your infinite love and mercy so that we may share that perfect inner peace which Christ brought, and the sure knowledge of everlasting life with You and all whom we love.
Amen.

Problems and Doubts

It used to be traditional for kindly old family doctors, as well as parents and grandparents, to console children and teenagers by telling them that their inexplicable aches and twinges were "growing pains". The phrase now gets applied to personal relationships: young husbands and wives learn more about one another and how to make a loving partner happy; a new employee or a new manager has to settle in to the work environment; it takes time to adjust to a new PC word-processor, or a whole new I.T. system of doing things at work or at home. Inevitably there are growing pains - but we get over them. Beginning a new religion, starting life again as a new Christian has growing pains too: but with God's help we cope with them and come through them. There are problems - but Jesus Himself had problems. The New Testament gives us a very vivid account of our Lord's temptations in the wilderness. In the Garden of Gethsemane, Jesus had to face the unimaginably terrible problem of death by crucifixion - but for our sakes He overcame everything. When doubts and fears threaten to overwhelm us, we turn to Him in prayer, and we remember the supreme example which He set for us. Through Him, we can do all things, overcome all things, solve all problems and survive our Christian growing pains in triumph.

Growing Pains

Nothing worth doing can ever be easy.
The war-song of triumph is written in pain.
"Forward!" and "Onward!" are only for warriors.
Blood on the field marks each mile that we gain.

Problems and doubts are built into the journey.
Tension and stress are just part of our fight.
Hold your torch high, and encourage your comrades:
Jesus is leading, and day follows night.

There is no retreat and there is no surrender.
Life is a battlefield: face it that way.
Christ will renew all your strength and your courage.
Jesus will bring us our Victory Day.

Prayer

Lord Jesus, You had doubts and temptations, and You overcame them all. You had problems which make ours seem trivial. Help us to get a proper sense of perspective. Remind us that Your wisdom is endless and unfathomable. Remind us that Your power is infinite, and that your eternal love for us exceeds even that vast wisdom and power. Lead us through all our problems, difficulties and doubts into your inner peace and eternal joy.

Amen.

Quiet Days and Retreats

There are as many equally valid ways to God as there are individual Christians. Some of us are powerful, zestful extroverts who thoroughly enjoy the world's many fights and challenges. We find a constant thrill in them. We are unashamedly ambitious. We relish controversy and the cut and thrust of heated argument. Other Christians are shy, quiet and gentle folk. They welcome tranquillity. God loves us all. He made us what we are: soldiers or shepherds; warriors or wayfarers. We are all His children. He wants us to be ourselves. There are some active, energetic Christians who find quiet days and retreats unbearably boring and regard them as a total waste of their time. They never go, and they do well not to go. Others find retreats and quiet days very helpful and spiritually nourishing. They go as often as they can, and they do well to attend. Racing cars cannot run along railway lines and Harley Davidsons do not give of their best in thick, wet rain-forests. But given the right conditions both perform superbly. We need to look at ourselves honestly and prayerfully. Let us talk to our Maker about the kind of people we *think* we are: He knows us infinitely better than we know ourselves. When with His help, we understand ourselves better, we will know whether retreats and quiet days are for us.

Peace

Peace within, the Saviour promised,
To all those who seek to be
Members of His Father's Kingdom,
And to serve Him faithfully.

Peace within, the Saviour offers,
Man or woman, young or old,
There is peace within His pastures,
There is safety in His fold.

Peace within, the Saviour grants us,
If disciples we will be.
Peace within and joy around us
Here and through eternity.

Prayer

Grant us Your peace, Lord, that we may grow to understand more and more of this Christian life to which You have called us. Help us to understand ourselves better so that we may know whether we are among those who will find help and renewal in retreats and quiet days. Whether we are active and outgoing by nature, or quiet and reflective, show us how we can best meet You in the innermost parts of our lives, and be renewed and refreshed by Your loving Presence there.
Amen.

The Christian Calendar

We live by times and seasons, the rhythms of the year. God comes to us through our calendars as surely as He comes to us in loving fellowship, prayer and worship. The seasons themselves teach us about God's promise of renewal and eternal life: the warmth and light of spring and summer come after the decay of autumn and the cold silence of winter. We celebrate Christ's triumph over death at Easter. We remember the coming of the Holy Spirit at Whitsun. We enjoy the wonderful festivities of Christmas when we celebrate Christ's incarnation in the stable at Bethlehem. There are many other Saints' Days and Holy Days scattered throughout the Christian year - a constant reminder that God is with us all the time. We can learn inspiring things from these Holy Feast Days, and from the lives of the Saints who set us such good examples. All these special spiritual occasions in the calendar help us to grow in the faith. But the Christian calendar will not keep its own special occasions. We have to play our part in making the most of Easter, Whitsun and Christmas. Human acts of love, fellowship, kindness and friendship to those in need are what God loves most. We cannot celebrate His Holy Days in any better way than by sharing them with others - especially those in the greatest need. That is what Christianises the calendar.

God's Calendar

Great Lord, You give us all our days.
Our moments come from You.
Help us to fill the calendar
The way You want us to.

Be with us in the summer sun
And our great winter feast.
Teach us to share our blessings with
The helpless and the least.

Guide us to give You back the days
Which You to us have given,
That Earth's good times may be the seeds
That grow and flower in Heaven.

Prayer

God of eternity, Master of times and seasons, help us to make the most of our Christian calendar. Teach us how to celebrate Christmas, Easter, Whitsun and all the other Holy Days in such a way that they help us to grow in faith and in our love for You and for one another. Teach us how to make every day a Holy Day by filling it with acts of love, kindness and generosity done in Your Name and for Your sake.
Amen.

Choirs and Church Music

Jesus told a very effective parable about a group of men who were given talents: most used theirs wisely and well -- but one did not. God gives each one of us talents: some Christians work hard to develop them and make the most of them - others don't. Talent is a tremendous responsibility - second only to freedom. It is a glorious gift - but it can also be a dangerous one. Part of the way that God reveals His love to us is that He trusts us with those two great responsibilities - ability and choice. He wants us to use our free will and our talents to help others, and to show our love to him by our love of those in need. Music is one of God's most generous gifts to His children. There is joy in writing it. There is joy in performing it. There is joy in hearing it. Great Christian music can transport us almost to the gates of Heaven, if we let it. We can share it in choirs and orchestras and in singing hymns and lively Gospel songs together. Music makes happiness and music makes friends. As we grow in faith and knowledge, we can think of God as the Supreme Composer and Conductor of the eternal and harmonious music of love. He has given each of us a part to play in that unending symphony. Our job, as we grow, is to learn from Him what our part is, and then to play it to the best of our ability for His sake.

Music

Christ told how talents, generously bestowed,
Were meant for us to use upon life's road.
If music is our gift: then let it flow
And echo angels' voices here below.
Composers and conductors show their art,
While orchestras and choirs play their part.
Transcendent music has a vital rôle:
Uplifts the mind and stirs the very soul.
Within its range sorrow and care depart
Peace, love and joy refresh the listening heart.
Within such music choirs of Heaven show
How their sweet echoes on the Earth may grow,
And as they lighten each and every load
God speaks to us through music's precious code.

Prayer

Most loving and generous God, You are the source of all that makes life good. All music comes from You, and we thank and praise You for this great gift. Help us to find You in the music we enjoy so much. Bless and inspire all those who have musical talent. Grant us the perception and sensitivity to appreciate all types of great Christian music so that it may draw us closer to You and to one another. We ask it in the name of Christ our Lord.
Amen.

Social Occasions

The Church's social occasions can be of great assistance to growing Christians -- and we can all help by contributing to them while we grow. There are special family services with chat and refreshments afterwards. There are quiz nights, bingo sessions, whist drives, keep fit groups, dances and discos. It's a pleasure to see the middle-aged organist who plays Bach and Mozart so well working as a DJ at the Church Youth Club on a Saturday night -- and the growing Christians among its members can learn a great deal about the true religious life from such an example. We need to get together with other Christians as often as we can in a relaxed, happy, informal, social atmosphere. There are three dangerous drains which can empty a church unless they are cemented over with love, fellowship and plenty of social events. The first gaping hole is cold, distant formality: the second is an artificial atmosphere of pretentious, pious religious silence when people would much rather talk freely to one another; and the third is a plethora of committees, regulations, hierarchies and trivial bureaucracies. The church's informal social occasions can provide powerful antidotes to this kind of nonsense. New Christians grow most vigorously and most happily when the church refreshes them with fellowship which is also good fun.

Having Fun Together

God is a God of joy and laughter:
There are no tears in His Hereafter.
While still on Earth, He'd have us be
Practising for Eternity.
A joke, a game, a smile, a song -
These help to move our world along.
A song, a joke, a game, a smile -
Can lighten many a weary mile.
And when in Heaven we take our place
Our Father has a smiling face.
While we've still earthly days to run
We'll serve our God by having fun.

Prayer

God of joy and Lord of laughter, we thank and praise You for the gifts of humour and fellowship. We thank and praise You for the fun which life can bring. Help us always to remember that You are the God of love and happiness, and that it is Your perfect will that we, your children, should be happy as well - here on Earth now, as well as in Heaven for all eternity. As we grow in the faith, help us to grow in happiness.
Amen.

Where to get Help and Advice

Whatever new thing we are learning, we have to begin at the beginning -- and we often need help. As growing Christians we need to know where to turn for help and advice on the many occasions when we need it. Thank God that there are several reliable places to which we can turn. He, Himself, is first and foremost. He is always more ready to listen than we are to pray. Then there are the Scriptures, where we can learn about others who have faced and overcome problems similar to our own. Fellow Christians who have been on the road a few years longer than we have are also a great source of help, comfort and spiritual strength - and they rejoice to be asked. The wonderful thing about helping our brothers and sisters along the way when they ask us to - and remember always that asking is a vital prerequisite: we should never offer advice that is not requested - is that working at a problem together helps both parties. By thinking lovingly and caringly about the problems of others, we can often solve our own. The best kinds of spiritual help are always natural, informal, spontaneous and unstructured. Elaborate church systems, rules, bureaucracies and hierarchies, provide either very poor answers, or no answers at all. There's a wise old saying which runs: "When we ask God for help, if He doesn't come Himself, He sends someone suitable."

Sources of Help

There are three places we can turn in need:
Our loving God who matches prayer with deed;
Then sacred words of Scripture, always there,
In which we find so much that lifts our care;
And other Christians on our pilgrim way,
Whose fellowship turns darkness into day.
The seeking and the asking must be ours:
God's gift of freedom gives us these great powers.
Unless we ask, our comrades will not know
We need their loving hands and hearts to show.

Prayer

Most loving and responsive Lord, kindest and most attentive Helper of all who are in need, be with us as we struggle to grow in the Christian faith because we do not always know where to turn for help. Teach us to come to You in prayer, as our first and greatest Resort. Illuminate the Scriptures for us, so that we may read them wisely and with understanding, and find great help and comfort in those sacred pages. Show us how best to ask our brother and sister Christians for help and advice, and grant us the grace to be able to help and advise others when they ask us. Amen.

A rich young ruler came to see Jesus to ask what was necessary to enter the Kingdom of God and achieve eternal life. Jesus asked him if he knew God's commandments. The young man answered that he had obeyed them scrupulously ever since he was a boy. Jesus told him that only one thing was lacking: "Sell what you have and give to the poor - and come and follow me." The New Testament records that the rich young ruler went away sorrowful because he had great possessions. Jesus remarked on how difficult it was for a rich man to enter the Kingdom of Heaven. As always, Jesus was absolutely right. If we allow money to use us - instead of using it to help the poor in our capacity as God's stewards - then our obsession with money may drive us away from God. The equal and opposite error occurs when we meet the dangerous notion that money is spiritually bad for us. It is nothing of the kind: the morbid desire for poverty is a greater evil than a lust for money. God wants us to work hard for those we love who depend upon our earning power: that's an inescapable Christian duty. We also need to earn enough to provide the necessities of life - and a few harmless pleasures and minor luxuries - *for ourselves as well.* What God requires of us, in addition, is to give all we can reasonably afford to help those in need.

The Christian Steward

What e'er I think I own, O Lord,
Nothing belongs to me.
This universe is Yours, great God,
In its entirety.

Please help me to remember this
In each decision made:
Wherever I may go, O Lord,
You own all that's displayed.

The sky, the stars, the Milky Way,
Each radiant galaxy:
Yet everything You make, O Lord,
You share so generously.

Please help me, Lord, to emulate
Your generosity,
And share with all who need my help,
What You have given me.

Prayer

Most loving Lord, Provider of all our earthly needs -- and far more - help us to be good stewards of such wealth and power as You have placed in our care at this time. May we use it not only wisely and well, but *generously*. Keep Your love ever before us, so that we may learn to enjoy giving to those in need, as You enjoy giving all things to us. Teach us that the giving of a smile, a kindly word of welcome, or a hand extended in friendship, is all part of our Christian stewardship.
Amen.

Other Faiths and Systems of Belief

In the course of my tutorial work, I meet many university students who have other faiths and systems of belief. We meet simply as fellow human beings with mutual affection and respect. Whether my friends are Muslims, Hindus, Buddhists, Sikhs, Jews, Baha'is or Pagans makes no difference at all to that affection and respect. If it did there would be something drastically wrong with me or with them. I believe absolutely and unequivocally that Jesus Christ is the only begotten Son of God in a very special and unique way. I believe in His Virgin Birth, His many miracles and His glorious Resurrection. I do not expect my friends who embrace other faiths to abandon their beliefs for mine -- any more than they would expect me to abandon Christ and join them. We are all brothers and sisters in God's eyes. We are all His children - but we're all *different*. We are all free to choose. We are all free to worship and serve Him and our fellow human beings in our own way. Love does not compel - it leads and invites -- and at the heart of every great faith is the certain knowledge that God is pure goodness, love and infinite mercy. If we as Christians hold up the light as we see it, and a brother or sister from another faith holds up a different torch, those lights do not hinder each other - they shine together to make the world a better and brighter place.

Together

God of knowledge, God of wisdom,
God of power, God of love,
All creating, all sustaining,
Lord of depths and heights above,
Help us so to love our brothers
And our sisters everywhere,
That we see Your Truth shine in them:
Broadest truth for all to share.

God of caring, God of sharing,
God of tolerance and peace,
God of all Your human children,
Bring us love and joy and peace.
Teach us to rejoice in difference,
Teach us how to understand:
You are God of all Your children,
You are Lord of every land.

Prayer

Lord of all, You alone understand every faith and system of belief. You alone know why these differences are here in our world. Help us to respect and tolerate those of our brothers and sisters who seek Your eternal truth by roads that are different from ours. Keep us faithful and steadfast in the Christian truth, revealed in Jesus, but grant us open minds and open hearts to welcome all our brothers and sisters, of whatever faith. Grant us the grace to understand that it is Your will for us to love and help all those who are in need, and to accept their love and help in return when we are in need. Teach us that it is how we treat one another that matters to You, and not our differences.
Amen.

Healing and Other Miracles

The idea of miracles can sometimes present problems for growing Christians, but we live in an unimaginably wonderful universe in which all things are possible.

Science tries to lay the tracks, but faith drives the train. God made us and everything around us. There are scientific laws and apparent sequences of cause and effect - but the most brilliant human researchers are still paddling in the shallows of God's infinite Ocean of Knowledge.

The limitless love of God generates healing and happiness for all of His children. Miracles of healing are an expression of God's love and power. Other miracles are, perhaps, a kind of short cut through what we think of as the natural world.

Computer wizards can reach deeper levels by using machine code, which goes straight to the heart of a problem and puts things right. Nature miracles may come about because Christ Himself, or one of God's special prophets or holy people, is using that great machine code which we call faith.

Miracles really do occur and our own progress towards God as growing Christians is one that we can all experience for ourselves.

Miracles

You are a miracle - and so am I.
The earth beneath our feet and starry sky
The fish that swim, the birds that fly above
Are miracles of God's creative love
The lame may walk again; the blind can see.
Christ's healing power is infinite and free.
God's glorious gifts around us gleam and shine:
His loving touch turns water into wine.
He breaks the bread of Life majestically
And multitudes are fed eternally
The Spirit comes to bless us -Holy Dove -
Whose gentle power makes mightiest mountains move.
God's miracles are there for all who try
To lift their thoughts from Earth to things on high.

Prayer

Lord of infinite power and wisdom, Maker of miracles, grant us that faith which Jesus taught, the faith which can move mountains. As we grow ever closer to You, help us to see the untold miracles of love, beauty and power which You spread around us in this wonderful universe. Amen.

Monitoring our Progress

Whether we're pumping iron in the gym, running a marathon or restoring a beautiful vintage Harley Davidson, we need to monitor our progress. Are we getting stronger ? Are we getting faster ? Is the bike getting closer to its pristine, showroom condition ?

So it is for growing Christians. We need to monitor our spiritual progress. Are we kinder, gentler, more thoughtful and less selfish than we used to be ? Are we more tolerant ? Do we care as much -- or even more -- for others than we care about ourselves ?

Unless we monitor our lives honestly and objectively, we won't make much spiritual progress. We need to see what's really inside our hearts. God is there to help us to improve and grow closer to Him.

Having a trusted friend, loved one, or partner, who cares enough to be honest as well as kind is a great help in this monitoring process. God's greatest gift is a loving family and friends.

Poem

I look into a glass and see
The shape and form whom I call "me".
I look around at sea and sky
And try to place this curious "I".
With all my weakness, fault and sin,
With "I" and "me" I must begin.
Though much is there which I can't see,
I study it objectively:
If there is some small goodness there,
God help me nurture it with care.
Though two steps forward - one step back -
God's love will hold us on the track.
There's so much more for us to mend:
But we ***shall*** get there in the end.

Prayer

God of perfect truth and absolute honesty, help us to monitor our progress. May we see our faults clearly, and improve them with Your loving help. May we recognise such small merits as we have, and do all in our power to make them grow.
Help us to examine our lives honestly and objectively so that we can increase our faith, goodness and love. Teach us how to find our faults, and grant us the strength and wisdom to become better people. For the sake of Jesus Christ our Lord. Amen.

God Helps us to Grow

Jesus said: "I am the Vine. You are the branches. Without me, you can do nothing."

He was, as always, absolutely right. Without Him we can do nothing: but the reverse is also true - with Christ we can do anything. He helps us to grow, to develop and to reach goals which were once beyond our wildest dreams.

It is impossible to set our sights too high. God's love and God's power are infinite. Yet the One who created and sustains His unimaginably vast universe is also vitally, tenderly and compassionately concerned with each individual man, woman and child. The more often we remind ourselves of that, the more surely will we grow as Christians.